Contents:

Part1
Developing A Whole School Strategy

Introduction   6
Reduction & Prevention   8
What is the Support Code?   9
What are Support Groups?   10
The Support Code in the Community   11
Stage 1 - staff to staff   12
Stage 2 - staff to pupils   13
Stage 3 - pupils to pupils   14
Stage 4 - development & sustainability   15

Maintaining Strategies   16

Part 2
Developing The Support Code   19

Introduction   20
Stage 1: Developing the Support Code in Class between Teachers and Pupils   22
Workshop 1   22
Workshop 2   23
Workshop 3   23

Stage 2: Developing the Support Code between Pupils   24
Workshop 1   24
Workshop 2   25
Workshop 3   26
Workshop 4   28

Stage 3: Development and Sustainability   31
Support Groups   33
Using the Curriculum   35

Appendix
Appendix 1: Forming the Circle   37

Appendix 2:
Active Displays and Support Certificates   39

Appendix 3:
Continuing the Support Code on a Daily Basis   40

Appendix 4:
Example of teacher and pupil responses to the initial code questions designed to develop a partnership between teacher and pupils   42

Appendix 5:
Example of pupil responses to the initial code questions designed to develop a partnership between the pupils
Childrens' responses   44
Legal framework   45
Useful contacts   46
Acknowledgements   47

GW00686402

"The Support Code is the most monumental intervention scheme the school has ever undertaken....the support code work has kept the human side of the curriculum in perspective and has helped to reinforce our behaviour code in an urban environment where all too often coldness lurks unabated."

John Snow – Deputy Head, Davies Primary School, Waltham Forest, London

"Well, I don't bully anyone and there are a lot of people that stopped bullying as well". (A Y5 child at Davies Primary School)

Years 5 and 8, pupils' views:

"Some people might stop hitting people. I like the idea and someone I know was getting bullied is not getting bullied anymore because of your work."

"It should go into all classes because it would teach children what to do in situations. Also children can help other children."

"It should do all the classes because it would help the children that bully."

"Because it is working with us so it should work with them."

"You should make the support code for the whole school because you can help each other."

"I think it is worth doing because it helps people stop bullying."

Teachers from Davies Primary in London and Tilbury Manor Primary, Essex:

- The support code is in its early stages and I believe if it is adopted as a whole school policy, it will be most beneficial to the whole school.
- The support code provides the opportunity for children to build their self-esteem in a very positive and worthy way.
- The code helps children to think about themselves in relation to others and the value of making their environment a safe place to learn and socialise.
- I honestly believe that the school would benefit from continuing the code. More teachers need to know exactly what to do to set up a support group and generally work through the role play and poster ideas.

Part 1

Developing A Whole School Strategy

Introduction

One need persistently expressed by young people in all surveys that listen to their voices is to be protected from bullying. Bullying impacts across physical, mental and emotional health, and rippling far beyond just the bully and victim.

The problem with bullying is how common it is. The really nasty forms of bullying, the kind that makes the newspapers, is much less frequent, fortunately, but thrives in an atmosphere where the "bullying tendency" is left unchallenged.

And what is this "bullying tendency"?

Some would say it's the cut and thrust of everyday life. It's how you make your way in the world. It's a by-product of the struggle to be successful and find self-purpose and meaning in life and therefore related to the pecking order. One gains power and acknowledgement through taking the power of others. Powerlessness drives this cycle which we all participate in. So, in the course of just one day, we can be a bully when trying to get our own way disregarding how others may feel; we can be a victim manipulated by others; we can collude in bullying through back-biting and gossip; we can stand by, with a "nothing to do with me attitude", or a fear that the bully's attention may be turned on oneself. In one survey (Brown 1992) 63% of children in one school who identified themselves as the victims of bullying, acknowledged that they bullied others.

It will remain remarkably difficult to work against the more extreme forms of bullying whilst we ignore opening up on the ways we want to be treated by others – and the ways we don't want to be treated. To ask such questions begins the strategy for challenging the bullying tendency.

Such questions allow us to explore our commonalities, especially those things when we think we're the only one stressing about various issues. They empower with a gentle inclusive equality, and building of empathy. They can eventually produce agreements around respect, mutual support and sympathy that have been built wholly by the participants. They are not bullied into behaving well to each other from someone in authority over them. These questions allow for the building of a model of bullying prevention: a "Support Code". There are no age or environmental limits on its use.

How did this code develop?

Dave Brown developed this code over many years of experience, teaching and working with young people to change the approach to bullying. With the national charity FSU Investing in Families, he worked on piloting a programme to reduce bullying. Later in his capacity as manager of the Youth Rising project in the London boroughs of Redbridge and Waltham Forest, he continued to develop this support strategy for schools. The Youth Rising project is a long term plan for promoting and improving the physical, mental and emotional health of the residents of the two London boroughs.

Developed by a series of staffroom and classroom workshops, the intention is to support schools in their ongoing efforts to build an environment and atmosphere of mutual, active and caring support and therefore oppose the bullying tendency. Locally and nationally there are now a number of schemes in place – peer mediation, peer counselling, buddying and circle time to name but a few – that are successfully challenging both teachers and students to examine the way they treat others.

A major feature of the support code, indeed the reason that the code was built, is the operation of peer support groups. Children and young people will support each other if they are helped in devising a structure that allows them to do it. The support groups are the main practical activity of the support code and details of their operation can be found in part 2.

The lessons we have learned from the pilot projects have been turned into a workshop programme, the details of which can be found within. The intention is to show the process and general direction that the support code strategy takes, and to give some indication of the time element. The process begins though with school staff building a support code for their own use before moving it into the classroom.

Youth Rising and Young Voice

A major strand of the philosophy of the Health Rising Strategy is towards inclusion and empowerment leading to prevention. This allows for the development of 'bottom-up' strategies in a variety of communal and institutional settings. Youth Rising was conceived as a way of ensuring that young people have a voice and are able to make a telling contribution to the way various services respond to their needs – needs identified by young people.

Young Voice has undertaken extensive consultations with young people across the two boroughs for the Youth Rising project, exploring social issues such as bullying, and its impact on young people's health and wellbeing. 104 young people gave preliminary interviews to determine the issues on which we should consult, and the 'Wassup?' questionnaire was developed and circulated among 13-26 year olds in 2002. There were 1,032 useable responses.
It is our belief that it is possible to protect the school community from bullying behaviours. It must be understood that this is a long-term strategy. There are no "quick fixes". Beginning the process however can have an immediate impact on the atmosphere in the school, and this is the start of change.

Dave Brown – Youth Rising
Adrienne Katz – Young Voice

The Youth Rising project sits within the Single Regeneration Budget (SRB).

The SRB is funded by the North East London Strategic Health Authority's long-term strategy for promoting the physical and emotional health of the resident, mental and emotional health of the residents of the two boroughs.

Issues

- Bullying is endemic in most, if not all, schools and communities.
- Being bullied, and bullying, is a common experience.
- Children who are bullied frequently truant, and consequently underachieve.
- Being persistently bullied leads inevitably to great stress for both the victimised child and, of equal importance, their family. The emotional impact and damage caused, frequently persists into adult life.
- Families as a whole can experience, in the local neighbourhood, the full range of bullying behaviours.
- Children who bully often become the prime targets for exclusion from school. Research indicates clearly that children with an unchecked bullying tendency easily slip into violent criminal behaviour in teen and adult life (Roland and Munth 1989, Elliot 1995).
- The most frequent response to bullying is based on a "find it - punish it" conflict model: a poor role model for arguing that "might is not right".
- There is a growing awareness that a punitive response to bullying is counter-productive. It does not challenge the bullying tendency.
- Any bullying prevention policy has to raise awareness, as well as devise, and maintain, effective strategies for both short and long term use.

Reduction and Prevention

- Any bullying prevention strategy must initially work to immediately assist those who are the focus of the bullying activity.
- Non-punitive strategies seek to include, help and empower all elements in the bullying situation. This means therefore the bullying and victimised, the colluders and bystanders. A partnership.
- A further partnership needs to be established between the various agencies, schools and groups working in the local community.
- No strategies can be effective unless the children/community as a whole are provided with the opportunity to take part in their construction and maintenance.
- The long-term goal is to establish a school/community environment where the action of bullying is made much more difficult because children and adults have established, and maintained, a sensitive awareness of the problems caused, and a willingness to act on the insights gained.

What is The Support Code?

What is...The Support Code?

The Support Code is...

- A bullying prevention strategy based on principles of self-help and inclusive group support.
- A bullying prevention maintenance strategy.
- A non-punitive strategy.
- A strategy challenging a bystanding philosophy and therefore capable of providing peer support in areas of need other than being a victim of bullying.
- Constructed through ownership, continuity and flexibility.
- Needs led rather than resource led. There are no strains on school budgets with normal training costs.
- Staff friendly. The code fits into the normal patterns of school pastoral and curriculum development and management.
- Consistent with, and seeks to develop, best practice models of both prevention of bullying and equal opportunity strategies.

In School, the Code can...

- Break the "conspiracy of silence".
- Provide both immediate and long-term support to both the victims of bullying and those who bully.
- Develop a proactive caring attitude between children.
- Provide multiple opportunities for children to take responsibility for their behaviour towards others.
- Help relationships between pupils and staff.
- Help staff help children in need.
- Help children help staff in need.

Between School and Home the Code can...

- Create and support the home/school partnership.
- Help resolve conflict between school and home.
- Allow and encourage, after appropriate training, active parental/carer participation in the prevention of bullying strategy.
- Allow, and encourage, the school, after appropriate training, to help resolve conflict between families.

The Support Code strategy seeks...

- Active caring/social agency partnerships and support. Schools and parents/carers cannot deal with bullying and related behaviours on their own.
- To move from a school based strategy into the local neighbourhood. It seeks to provide local neighbourhood volunteer support to families who are being harassed racially or otherwise.

What are Support Groups?

The No-Blame approach to bullying shows conclusively that children will support each other when given the opportunity to do so. It became clear in practice that children are keen to partner with others to support children, given the opportunity, in any area of need. Initial impetus for the Support Code grew out of thinking through strategies for supporting and maintaining the work of No-Blame and general support groups.

In the school, Support Groups are...

- A practical and immediate mechanism for supporting children and staff who find themselves in need of help. This is not limited to anti/prevention of bullying support.

- An immediate response to, and partnership with, parents/carers who have approached the school with bullying or other concerns.

- A practical and caring response to bullying or disruptive children.

- Recognition that, often, the people best placed to help children in need, are other children.

- An inclusive strategy allowing all children the opportunity of joining in with helping others in need.

- Empowering: support strategies are devised by support group members. Groups are facilitated by a trained adult, older pupil or teacher and monitored by the key member of teaching staff.

- An additional strategy for anti-bullying policies. Support groups compliment other strategies including peer counselling, peer mediation, Circle Time and the No-Blame approach.

- Entirely non-punitive.

and encourage...

- The continual development of empathy, sensitivity and general caring skills amongst children and staff.

- A raised and maintained level of awareness with regard to one's behaviour towards others.

- The taking of personal responsibility: No Bystanders.

- Proactive and sympathetic partnerships between parents/carers, children, school staffs and caring agencies.

- Curriculum and pastoral developments.

but do not

- Interfere with child protection measures and procedures, but may have a positive supporting role as part of an ongoing strategy to support a child, and family, in both school and neighbourhood.

- Break rules of confidentiality. At base level, children and adults need only know that a child is in need of friendly support. Where formal child protection is not an issue, the focus of the group will reveal only what they choose to the group facilitator.

It should be noted that children needing support do not meet with the selected support group, as a group, at any stage unless they choose to do so. Where possible, it is intended that the parents/carers ask for support for their child and discuss possible helping strategies. If this is not possible, then the group facilitator fulfils this role.

The Support Code in the Community

- An essential feature of the code strategy is the intention to change the atmosphere in the school so that bullying, and related behaviours, occur with a diminishing frequency.

- The school is not the only environment where bullying takes place. The local neighbourhood can also experience endemic bullying.

- Bullying occurs in the local community in a number of guises. Amongst these can be found racial harassment; neighbour conflicts; neighbourhood gossiping; gangs; sexism; homophobia; culture/religious prejudices etc.

- Attitudes and behaviour being played out by children in school are frequently a reflection of what is being taught to them, and what they are experiencing in the home and local community.

- Bullying begun in the neighbourhood is often continued in school.

- Bullying begun in the school is often continued in the neighbourhood.

- The experience of being bullied provokes feelings of fear, isolation and confusion. This is not related to age. Adults experience as large a depth and range of emotions as young people.

- Communities face similar difficulties to schools in combating bullying. Prevention of bullying strategies in the community must seek to challenge bystanding behaviours as well as provide neighbour support.

- Schools are one of the centres of the local community. A prevention of bullying partnership between the two would have mutual benefits.

- Schools and their local communities cannot work in isolation. Any such partnership would need the collaboration of local social/caring agencies.

- The support code is a strategy for building and maintaining such a partnership. It operates by participants building a neighbourhood support strategy.

- It is a "bottom-up" approach. Inclusivity and enabling are key elements of the code. It is a process that is facilitated rather than led.

- Under the developing code a network of neighbourhood support volunteers needs to be organised. This is intended to combat the fear and isolation experienced either because a member of the family is experiencing bullying in a specific environment, or the family as a whole are suffering from some form of harassment.

- The role of local agencies, via the developing code, is to work together to support, and initiate, work with the local schools and community.

Stage 1:

Staff to Staff – Staffroom Workshops: External and Internal Facilitation

Aims

- To introduce the support code strategy.
- To help the staff team develop a mutually supportive and caring environment.
- To help the staff team develop strategies for maintaining and renewing a mutually supportive and caring environment.
- To prepare teaching staff for the work with the pupils in the classroom.
- To enhance emotional literacy and spark emotional intelligence.

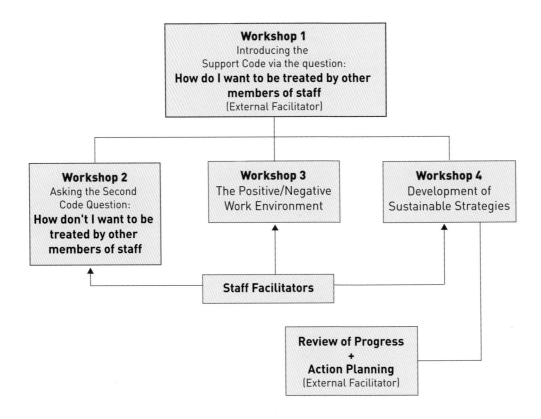

Stage 2:

Staff to Pupils – Classroom Workshops - Teacher Facilitated

Aims

- To begin the development of the code in the classroom.
- To enhance emotional literacy and spark emotional intelligence.
- To introduce the concepts of inclusivity, ownership and partnership.
- To begin the practice of inclusivity, ownership and partnership.
- To produce the first code statements expressing the needs of teacher and pupils.

Workshop 1
Presentation of, and discussion on, the teacher's Wish List based on answers to the initial code questions:
What do I want from my pupils?
What can they expect from me?

The production of an agreed list

Workshop 2
Presentation of, and discussion on, the teacher's Wish List based on answers to the initial code questions:
What do I want from my teacher?
What can s/he expect from me?

The production and display of an agreed list

Workshop 2
Teacher/Class design of code statements display materials based on the agreed lists compiled in the first two workshops.
In-class presentation of the display materials followed by mounting of the materials for display inside, and outside, the classroom.

Stage 3:

Pupils to Pupils – Classroom Workshops - Teacher Facilitated

Aims

- To begin the process intended to lead to the prevention of bullying.
- To enhance emotional literacy and spark emotional intelligence.
- To generate the first pupil-pupil code statements.
- To generate the first pupil-pupil practical and active non-punitive strategies of care.
- To generate more display materials.

Workshop 1
- Asking of the initial code question:
  How do I want to be treated by other people in my class?
- Division into groups to examine the meanings of the sentiments expressed and to devise slogans

    (Code Statements)

- Presentations

Workshop 2
- Discussion/examples of the **practice** of code statements
- Group work on solutions/strategies
- Presentation of group work
- Generation of code action statements
- Display of action statements and guides for practising the strategies referred to for **doing** action statements

Workshop 3
Second Code Questions:
- **How don't I want to be treated by others?**
- **How shouldn't I treat others?**

    Process as for workshop 1

Workshop 4

Developing Strategies and Action Statements:

    Process as for workshop 2

Stage 4:
Development and Sustainability

Aims

- To allow the code strategy to develop a proactive atmosphere of inclusive mutual care and mutual safety.
- To encourage the continual growth of emotional literacy and intelligence.
- To sustain, in the long term, a proactive atmosphere of inclusive mutual care and mutual safety.

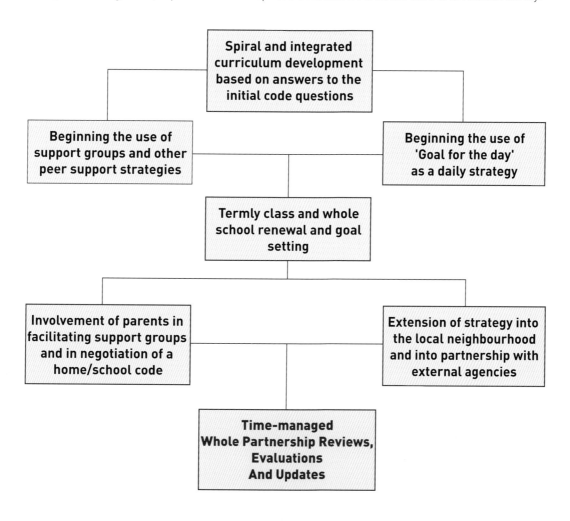

How do we maintain strategies?

Many schools now have a developed awareness that children and young people have to be protected from bullying. Indeed there is a legal framework obliging them to do so. The problem such schools face is how to maintain strategies in the long-term. The development and consequent piloting of a pupil-pupil support code has been designed to meet this need.

The strategy of developing such a code has grown out of reactive though non-punitive, anti bullying policies, and the need to sustain them long-term. This is Bullying Prevention. Raising awareness of bullying issues in a school is relatively easy in comparison to long-term maintenance of practical preventative strategies. Failure to maintain awareness and deploy sustainable strategies means that bullying will creep back into the underground of any school even if initial strategies seem to make progress.

Empathy and open communication lead to a healthier emotional life

It is not the purpose of the support code to provide a list of rules, nor a suffocating form of peer group pressure, but rather to facilitate the development of empathy and open communication: a mutual assertiveness where "no" is taken to mean "no" and not resented. An ideal world really, at least from the victim's perspective – and most other people's as well.

What prevention of bullying strategies must do is make the world a nicer place to live in. How do we do that? If the child world can be a frightening place, wait until the adult world comes along! The pressures we put on each other makes occasional bullies, colluders, bystanders or victims out of each of us, and even the long-term victimised can find ways to join in this.

Most of the time, for most of us, it is unintentional. We still hurt others though, but not as much as the hurt and anguish that is caused when someone has let their feelings for others get damaged, or remain underdeveloped, to the extent that they target someone as their victim. Sometimes groups do this as well.

Value in the process itself

Besides providing the practical outcomes of the code itself, the process of developing the strategies allows for, indeed insists upon, the open and unfettered discussion of values. Children and young people are being asked how they want to be treated, and how they think they should treat others. It is not possible to do such work, or maintain an impact, without discussing values or their social contradictions. The prime value to be discussed, and the implications examined, concerns mutual and inclusive supportive actions without losing individuality, the ability to be creative, or self-improvement ambitions.

Pupil ownership

The pupils have an essential control over the development of the code, including the strategies for both implementing and maintaining it, though it has a boundary that is non-punitive. Teachers have the responsibility of facilitating the code's development, and, via the curriculum, of supporting it: a partnership. Obvious, and democratic, development would include a teacher to pupil code, a staff to staff code and a school to carer code.

Values

If we are to take the prevention of bullying seriously, rather than as "flavour of the month", and develop and maintain long-term strategies, then we have to find a way to develop values, both in our children as well as ourselves, which challenge the bullying, colluding and bystanding attitudes. Since we are concerned with the prevention of bullying, then it is necessary that such values are not imposed. We cannot tell children and young people what to think, and then punish them for not responding as we would wish them to: this is bullying behaviour and therefore a poor role model for pupil co-operation in preventative strategies. Indeed it is a poor role model for pupil co-operation in **any** form of behaviour policy.

The root of building and maintaining bullying prevention strategies is to **explore** the value of people being nicer to each other. This journey certainly has guides, but not leaders: facilitators not trainers.

Examining our own stance as adults with power

When a school first begins to develop anti-bullying policies and strategies, the way forward seems clear enough. To lessen bullying, ensure the pupils know it will be reacted to with severity; encourage bystanders to break the conspiracy of silence and let you know that bullying is occurring; ensure that victimised children are both protected as well as taught how to avoid being bullied, perhaps through assertiveness training.

The values seem obvious enough: aggression, intimidation and violence will not be tolerated. Yet herein lies a contradiction: we say that to use your might against someone weaker than you is wrong, but, because of the ethos of punishing the bullying child's aggression, we have to use our might in order to contain or eliminate the problem. Frequently, like the bullying child, we find that an implied threat is a good first action: we try to scare the bully into inactivity.

The counterproductive contradiction

For some people working in bullying prevention, this has become too much of a contradiction. Indeed some would describe "bullying the bully" as being somewhat

hypocritical and largely counter-productive, not only in terms of responses to bullying children/young people but also in the message that this gives to **all**. It does not challenge bullying behaviour at its root but rather simply suppresses it until attention is focused on some other area of school life, and can do little to raise awareness of the parts all children, young people and adults, play in the victimisation of others, or how easy it is to become the target for the aggression of others.

The power of 'fitting in'

It is easier to join in bullying, or ignore it, rather than dispute or challenge. None of us likes to admit, perhaps even to ourselves, that we participate in such behaviours. We teach the ideal, but our behaviour all too frequently describes the reality of colluding in bullying that we have not challenged in ourselves. No wonder teachers and carers can find the direct teaching of values such a difficult task. We all succumb to the imposition of values, yet we all contribute to the uncritical encumbrance of values onto others. We want our children, to "fit in", because we know what can happen to those who don't.

This common fear is an indication of the endemic nature of low-level bullying, and is the atmosphere to be changed at all levels if more aggressive bullying behaviours are to be effectively challenged.

It's not enough to say 'no"

If this then describes the problem, how may it be addressed? Perhaps the first step is to recognise that punitive responses to bullying behaviours, necessarily and rightly focused on protection for the victimised child, cannot, alone and long-term, prevent children, young people or adults, from bullying each other. It is not enough to say "no!" with clout!

Pupil driven or imposed on pupils?

We have to attend to the root of the problem. Bullying prevention strategies are at their most fruitful when they seek active co-operation through enhanced and open communication. This is assumed to mean between teachers and pupils, and this is certainly of fundamental importance, as is the quality of communication between child and carers, and carers and the school. However, the **key** communication has to be between the children and young people themselves, yet this is an area easily overlooked. It is vital for successful long-term bullying prevention strategies that children and young people open up to each other, and are helped in that process by their teachers and carers.

Schools can adopt strategies that actively and positively seek to raise **and maintain** the general awareness, sensitivity and thoughtfulness of the whole school community. An essential part of the process, if it is not to stifle creativity and individuality and create an intimidating atmosphere, is that it must be pupil driven, and pupil owned, but adult facilitated, and must make provision for the needs of **all** the pupils. These are the reasons for developing the concept and ideals of the support code strategy. The code is an umbrella under which differing support strategies can be developed and inclusively applied.

"If we don't have kindness, there would be loads of fights in the classroom and everyone would be hurt and nobody will be friends, and nobody will be happy."

How do we want to be treated?

"With respect. Everyone has a right to be respected. We are all humans and should respect others - even people we do not like."

Part 2

Developing The Support Code

A teacher's search for a way to move from 'anti-bullying' work to 'prevention of bullying'

This handbook is intended as a guide for the initial stages of code development in the school by the class/form teacher. The workshops contained within, and fully described and planned, began development in a Boys secondary school in the East London borough of Waltham Forest. It was wonderful for me, as a pastoral manager in the school, to see how the students across all year groups, including those identified as "bullies", were prepared to support each other when given the formal opportunity to do so through the operation of voluntary support groups (please refer to page 33).

From reaction to prevention

It was the success of the support groups that led me to try to find a way to sustain them as an integral part of any school's pastoral management. Leaving my school, I worked within and with a number of primary, secondary and special schools over a number of years eventually leading to the development of the fully-fledged support code. In the end it was about a search which led from reaction to prevention. From simply having to react to bullying when discovered - anti-bullying, (hard enough to do and even harder on the victimised) the developing code was an attempt to creating and sustaining an atmosphere of empathy and mutual support – bullying prevention.

It had to be founded on emotional literacy and intelligence with skilled external to school agency support for those who find it difficult to change emotional habits that lead them to oppress others.

Embedded into the life of the school community

Once embedded into the life of the school community, it is then that community's responsibility to continue to develop the code and keep it alive. This handbook, particularly in the appendices, gives some suggestions on how to do this on a daily basis, particularly in the primary school. All strategies have been piloted in all sectors, however I would anticipate that each school, and class/year group, discover further ideas to trial as they grow the code.

No added workload

Establishing the code doesn't mean an increase in teacher workload but it does suggest different ways of working because of its co-operative nature: teachers cannot bully pupils or each other, and pupils cannot bully teachers or each other. It will, and should, have an impact on general classroom behaviour as well as other discipline/management issues that every school faces. It should enhance educational attainment through pupils not having to stress about personal safety.

Sustainability though, over years, can be lost amongst change, new staff and the yearly change in pupils. The only "constants" are the curriculum, pupils going through the school and the desire of teachers to give their students the best education they can in a safe environment. The willingness of teachers and other school staff to work with students on their safety and health can be taken for granted, and the curriculum is, with imagination, a flexible beast (please refer to page 35 "Using the Curriculum").

Sustaining the work – the real challenge

Sustaining a whole-school bullying prevention strategy is difficult – perhaps more so in the secondary sector where teachers see a much larger proportion of students through the week than their primary colleagues. Primary staffs have much more contact time with a smaller group of pupils and are able therefore to more easily pick up on when a child is unhappy. It is also comparatively easier at primary level for a teacher to mould the class as a whole into a mutually supportive and emotionally literate group. I found the difference in contact time a major boost to support group and code development when I taught in the primary sector.

However I also found that students in Y10+Y11 were quite happy supporting pupils, both in their own and in lower year groups. A key of course is to develop processes/strategies that can cross sectors and this means secondary and primary teachers and pupils working together. Having worked in and with both sectors, I realise how much each has to offer the other. Beginning to look together at bullying prevention around transition would be a good starting point.

The important transition age

Most of the exercises here are pitched at the transition age including years 5 ,6 ,7 and 8, but are simple enough in concept to be modified for any age group or situation. I have attempted to provide an explicit guide to each exercise including the reasons for it and what you should be looking to get out of it. This book is not written for the specialist teacher but for all teachers, so they can work together on these issues with confidence.

I hope you find this book useful whichever education sector you are in and whatever your post is.

Stage 1:

Developing the Support Code in Class between Teachers and Pupils

This begins the strategy of developing the support code in the classroom. The intention is to start at the first meeting with a new class. However, it can also be developed after any half or full term holiday. It can also be used to negotiate a new relationship between teacher and class when there are difficulties. This forms an essential element of the code for the following reasons:

● Where teacher leads, pupils will follow. Teachers being open and explicit about how they want things to be, and why, will encourage pupils to do the same. This is especially true for circle time and "Goal for the Day". (Please refer to the "Goal for the Day" scheme on page 31.)

● Teachers should never ask pupils to do what they are not prepared to do. If we want children and young people to work in partnership to support each other, then the same ethos should prevail between pupils and teacher.

● It begins the development of a positive, inclusive and solution focused atmosphere.

● It presents the method to pupils in an unusual way that tends to capture interest.

● It allows the teacher to experience facilitation – important when developing the code between pupils.

● It produces the first negotiated agreements.

● It produces the first active displays. (Please refer to "Active Displays and Support Certificates" – Appendix 2 page 39.)

The Process

All parts of the support code partnership begin with similar questions, the "initial code questions", being asked, so...

Workshop 1.

● **Before meeting with your pupils, ask yourself,** "What can/should pupils in my class expect from me"?

● **Also ask yourself,** "What do I want from pupils in my class"?

● **Draw up a list in answer to these questions** (An example is provided in Appendix 4 page 42.)

● **Keep the list to A4 size. This is so your answers can be displayed in a number of strategic places both inside the classroom and on the door and walls outside the classroom. This display should not go up until you have discussed your list with your class.**

● **Form the circle. It would be useful to have the chairs ready in a circle.** (Please see, "Forming the Circle", Appendix 1 page 37.)

● **Tell your pupils what you have done, why you are doing it and read out your list.**

● **Allow limited discussion on the list. Remember though that it is your list and it is what you want as a teacher. Your side of the partnership is to deliver effective teaching within a secure and safe environment and your list should reflect this.**

● **Discuss with the pupils the places your list could be displayed to remind both you and them of your side of the partnership.**

● **Select pupils to put them up immediately and close the circle after telling the pupils that the circle will be reformed after lunch so they can have their turn at saying what they want from you, and what you can expect from them.**

Workshop 2.

Separating the two bits of code questions is useful for a number of reasons. Firstly, the reformed circle is a reinforcement of the circle rules. Secondly, it allows the teacher to reassert the supportive, open and disciplined atmosphere that is the goal. Thirdly, it should help ensure that when pupils answer the code questions, they will do so thoughtfully after the example of the morning session.

- Allow the pupils to move furniture if that is necessary for forming the circle.
- Form the circle and begin by reminding pupils of the rules of the circle, and why the rules are there.
- Tell the pupils that it is now their turn to say what they want from you. Make sure you tell them **why** they are being asked to do this.
- Ask the question, "What do you want me to do for you?" or similar. Try to make sure, without undue pressure, that every pupil provides a response. Let them know they can give the same answer as someone else if they want. This is part of making the circle safe.
- Record the answers.
- Allow some discussion on the answers.
- Ask the question, "How do you think you should behave towards me?" **or similar.**
- Record the answers.
- Allow some discussion on the answers.
- Close the circle.
- Print their answers onto A4 paper and display next to your answers. (An example of pupil responses to these questions can be found in Appendix 5 page 43.)

Workshop 3.

Display is an important part of code development because:

- It is a reminder of what is trying to be achieved.
- It is a visual reminder of agreements made.
- It encourages sustainability of code action ("doing") statements showing that the code is not something just talked about.

- Using differing art materials and mediums, have the pupils generate a display based on their own answers to how they want to be treated by you, and what they expect from you.
- Generate your own display based on your answers to what you expect from them and what they can expect from you.
- Mount both sorts of display both in and outside the classroom.

Intended Outcomes
- To open the partnership of safety and learning between teacher and pupils.
- To introduce the concepts of negotiation and mediation.
- To introduce the concept of mutual support inherent in partnerships.
- To enhance the building of emotional literacy and intelligence.
- To introduce the teacher to facilitation.
- To introduce the teacher to classroom management under the support code. (Please refer to Appendix 3, page 40 "Continuing the Support Code on a Daily Basis".)

Stage 2:

Developing the Support Code between Pupils

If you have participated in the initial development of the staff to staff code and begun the teacher to class code, then you should have some idea of what is coming next!

- The process for beginning the code is the same in each case, with the initial code questions asked being variations on a theme depending on which partnership is being formed.
- In this case the partnership is between the pupils. You, as teacher, are the facilitator of this process.
- Facilitating is different from teaching. Your role is to keep the pupils focused and help them take responsibility for building the code.
- This first part of the code is about raising awareness rather than the building of strategies.
- It is also about providing a climate where pupils are encouraged to be open and honest about their feelings. This is a particular reason that the use of circle time is encouraged.

The Process

It is important to note that the words and phrases arising in this workshop (as in Workshop 3) provide the curriculum input for future investigations. (Please refer to "Using the Curriculum" page 35.)

Workshop 1

- Form the circle, and remind the class of the circle time rules (Please see "Forming the Circle" at Appendix 1 page 37.)
- Ask the question, "How do you want to be treated by the other pupils in your class"?
- Try to ensure that all pupils give an answer, but don't put pressure on to answer, and don't allow the other pupils to pressurise. Make sure pupils know that they can give an answer that another pupil has given.
- Record all answers – initially on a black/white board etc, but eventually in note form. These answers form the basis for later curriculum work.
- When the circle has completed their answers, unravel some of them. For instance: if an answer is, "Treat me with respect", then ask what does "respect" actually mean? The reason for this is to begin to emphasise that the support code is about doing.
- Explore the words that the children have come up with. **Try to stress the commonality of the answers. There are many positive aspects to children, young people and adults, hearing that others feel the same way.**
- Give the pupils individual/group work allowing them to create posters, slogans, poems etc. based on the words they have suggested. Give this part of the work a reasonable time limit. Encourage them to make the designs colourful, as it will be used for display both in and outside the classroom.
- When completed, have the pupils present their work to the class explaining why they have done what they have done.
- Generate slogans for display.
- Mount and display the work.

Intended Outcomes

- Pupils begin to listen to each other and become more open in expressing their feelings thereby enhancing emotional literacy and intelligence.

- Children enjoy doing the posters etc. and presenting them to the rest of the class.

- Teachers and children from other classes will look at the growing display work outside the classroom. (Please refer to Appendix 2 page 39, "Active Displays and Support Certificates".)

Workshop 2:

Developing the Support Code Building Blocks

The "building blocks" are the words and phrases given in response to the initial code questions. The intention is to unravel some of them. A simple word like "respect" has a number of different meanings each surrounded by differing contexts. The trick is to tease out meanings that are commonly owned, and then devise complimentary slogans that become active displays/code action statements. A suggested method follows, but first there are other aspects to this piece of work to consider...

- It maintains and builds upon work done in the first workshops.
- It is designed to help pupils think in a supportive framework.
- It marks the beginning of helping pupils to evolve and own practical, supportive and caring strategies for helping each other.
- It emphasises the taking of responsibility for one's actions – or lack of them!
- It allows all pupils to explore, and practice in a safe environment, some situations that require them to actively help, with a practical emphasis, somebody in need.
- It allows pupils to explore their own feelings and the emotions of others.
- It is the initial vehicle from which the action/code statements will emerge.

The Process

The intention here is to help all pupils empathise with the needs of others via an exploration of pupil prioritised words/phrases elicited from the initial code questions. It is where the words/phrases get turned into role-playing action.

- Form the circle and remind the class of the circle time rules.
- Ask each pupil to choose a word/phrase from the display of the initial code questions and say what appeals to them about the word/phrase. Allow no discussion at this point to encourage each pupil to attempt an answer. Make sure answers are recorded for all to see.
- Facilitate pupils discussing an order of priority. If an order can be agreed, though it is not important to do so, this also needs recording.
- Split the class into groups of 3/4.
- Ask each group to choose a word/phrase from the circle time list. Give a few minutes for this and then ask each group which word/phrase they are going to explore, and the reason for their choice.
- Set the groups to devise a role-play around the word/phrase that both explores a problem and offers a solution that does not involve the use of force. Some examples should be given at this point. The easiest is a bullying scenario where the problem is a bully, but the solution cannot involve kicking the bully's head in!
- Let the groups know they will be presenting to the rest of the class.
- Only give the groups 15 minutes to decide on their scenario, consider their solutions and prepare their presentations.
- After each presentation, allow the class to discuss differing solutions.
- **Any and all class agreements concerning realistic solutions should be recorded and displays made of agreed action statements and guides for doing action statements.**

Intended Outcomes

- To continue the development of empathy.
- Development of listening and hearing skills.
- Developing understanding of words and concepts being explored.
- Pupils beginning to understand the nature of responsibility to others.
- Pupils beginning to understand potential consequences of poor behaviour towards others.

Workshop 3

The code is intended as a positive, though realistic, process leading to a school atmosphere of reciprocal supportive actions between pupils, between school staff, and between pupils and school staff. The first code question, framed in positive terms, asked how the pupils wanted to be treated by each other. This workshop takes on the negative side of that question because...

- To ignore the negative side would only give/show half the emotions at play.
- As with the first code question, commonality of answers given point to commonality of stresses, leading to the subject of security of partnership in solutions.
- It gives pupils the opportunity to be heard without laying blame or with fear of reprisal.

The Process

The same model as for the first code question, but with a difference on emphasis. So...

- Form the circle, and remind the class of the circle time rules.

- Ask the question, "How don't you want to be treated by other pupils in your class"?

- Try to ensure that all pupils give an answer, but don't put pressure on to answer, and don't allow the other pupils to pressurise. Make sure pupils know that they can give an answer that another has given.

- Record all answers – initially on a black/white board etc, but eventually in note form. These answers form the basis for later curriculum work.

- Unravel some of the emotions involved by asking some pupils, "How does it make you feel when someone does something to you that you don't like?"

- Also ask, and explore, how someone who causes misery to others might feel.

- Ask the pupils to put up their hands, no discussion, if they have ever helped anyone needing help.

- Ask the pupils to put up their hands, no discussion, if they have ever made anyone miserable, or bullied someone.

- Again, try to stress the commonality of the answers.

- Explore the words that the pupils have come up with.

- Give them work allowing them to create posters, slogans, poems etc. based on the words they have done. Give this part of the work a reasonable time limit.

- Encourage them to make their work colourful, as it will be used for display both in and outside the classroom.

- When completed, have the pupils present their work to the class explaining why they have done what they have done.

- Mount and display the work.

Intended Outcomes

- Staff and pupils becoming more sensitive to the needs of others.

- A growing awareness that causing pain to others is not fun for them.

- Pupils listening to, and hearing, each other.

- Pupils enjoy doing the posters etc. and presenting them to the rest of the class.

- Staff and pupils from other classes will look at the growing display work outside the classroom. (Please refer to Appendix 2 page 39, "Active Displays and Support Certificates".)

- Pupils become more thoughtful in their behaviour towards each other and adults.

- Adults become more thoughtful in dealing with conflict – either between pupils or between pupils and themselves. (Please see Appendix 3 page 40, Continuing the Support Code on a Daily Basis".)

Workshop 4

This workshop is intended to provide a process model for developing new code strategies and statements at future points. The book can never be closed in that new issues arise, and old issues need to be revisited. Strategies and statements are not sacrosanct. They are open to challenge and change. The essence of safety and security is that each person takes responsibility for not hurting another intentionally. When children reach this point of understanding, the code has begun to take hold. It is useful to constantly ask, "Who's responsibility to do?" when discussing strategies of care.

Once this workshop has taken place, all the initial foundations of the code are in place except for the development of support groups. (Please see page 10 - "Support Groups".) Code statements are derived from code strategies and are intended as a reminder in that...

- They are the surface of any given agreed strategy, a stated portion of the overall policy of the inclusive enhancement of emotional literacy and intelligence and the quality of life.
- They are action statements.
- It is easy for both staff and pupils to forget what has been agreed to try.
- They are active displays, and the most important.
- They are the basis for future development of the code strategies and spiral curriculum development.
- They should form part of the welcome for new pupils and staff to the school. (Please refer to Appendix 3 page 40, "Continuing the Code on a Daily Basis".)

Examples of Code Statements

These come from a Y6 class who had gone through the code process:

- No bystanding. Everybody agreed that other children could, and should, intervene if there was a problem between some children. No violence can be used - either physical or mental. If children can't sort it out, then the teacher must be told. When a problem is sorted out, the teacher should also be told.
- Everyone agreed that if there is a problem, i.e. someone is bothering you, then you must try to find the courage to speak up to the teacher. If you can't speak up, then someone must take the responsibility of doing it for you.
- If you are seen as being the source of the problem, you have to listen and talk about it in a calm manner.
- The best way to avoid trouble is not to start something yourself. If nobody started anything then nobody would get hurt.

As can be seen, the strategies are embedded in the statements. They are **action** statements. To be explicit, they are **doing** statements. That is why they have to be agreed and owned by the pupils. The staff role is very much that of facilitation and support, but also that of making sure that the final word version reflects the pupils understanding at **that** point. The code is intended to evolve!

The Process

- Form the circle
- Refer to and read every slogan on the walls, and see if children can remember what has been put outside the classroom.
- Discuss with them what the slogans mean.
- Tell the pupils that words are all well and good, but that actions are what count (or some verbal derivative!). Tell them this is to be a "how to" session.
- Choose one of the slogans to provide an example, or make one up so that the pupils have a full range of their choices to work from. A slogan, devised by children, was "It's cool to be kind." Firstly what does it mean "to be kind"? and, secondly, how can "being kind" be put into practice? What is the first small step that has to be taken? That first "small step" is the beginning of applying the code in practice.
- Choose one of the proposed strategies offered by your class as solutions to the conflict and care scenarios they have been exploring.
- Explore with the pupils the **doing** parts of the proposed strategy. **Who** had to do **what**?

- Help the class come up with, and agree, an action statement for the strategy that **accurately** reflects what the pupils are saying had to happen to solve the scenario problem.
- Where possible, encourage the word "please" to begin the statement (unlike the above examples!). The statements are **not** a set of rules: they **are** about how to actively care and support.
- Discuss the statement with the class, pointing out that it is an **action/doing** statement.
- Ask the class for a goal for the day (please refer to page 31) that allows the statement to become active. Does the statement bear on any class issue? What small steps, in relation to the action statement, can be made?
- Agree the strategy for making the goal. If, for instance, less aggression is the general goal based on the scenario problem, then the goal could be that everybody remembers to say "please" and "thank you" to each other when wanting something from somebody else. Small steps always!
- Move the pupils into groups to devise further code statements and strategies.
- Either as an ending to the workshop, or as an additional workshop, have pupils present their work, negotiate agreement over the strategies with the other pupils and mount displays both in and outside the classroom.
- When there are enough strategies available, they should be put into a small booklet for pupils and staff. The strategies are a semi-permanent display, but will be added to as the code develops.

As with all the code work, this is intended as a repeatable exercise, specifically designed in this case to generate code action statements. The source for code statements will in future come from issues raised in circle time and classwork, rather than pupils having to repeat the earlier processes of code work. However, it may be useful to use earlier parts of the work to refresh and move on. Mix and match and introduce your own ideas!

... but please stay focused on the inclusive and supportive nature of the goal – to build and maintain, in ownership and partnership with the pupils, an environment of safety and security that enhances the quality of life for all.

Intended Outcomes

● All children begin to take responsibility for devising and agreeing strategies of support and care.

● All children begin to take responsibility for applying the agreed strategies, and are encouraged and helped in doing so by staff.

● Pupils enjoy the process of getting to the first statements and devising initial strategies.

● Pupils and staff encourage and support each other in practising and using the strategies.

● Active displays

● A positive and discernible small-step change in behaviour and attitude.

● Pupils are ready to join support groups. (Please refer to page 33.)

Stage 3:

Development and Sustainability

This is an ongoing stage with new strategies, such as Support Groups and Goal for the Day, being introduced. Also looked at here will be the curriculum enhancements that necessarily underpin the emotional literacy and intelligence developments being sought.

(a) "Goal for the Day"

This easy to use, and highly effective, strategy comes out of the use of circle time/class meetings. A central function of circle time is to create an atmosphere of safety and security where pupils are encouraged to raise issues of concern to them, and have the other participants hear what they are saying. "Goal for the Day" allows the issues discussed to be turned into practical class agreement for action on a daily basis. This in turn allows the support code to be developed and maintained also on a daily basis.

- The time element in this is 10 minutes at the beginning and end of each day. Circle time rules apply, but it is not necessary to rearrange the classroom furniture. The strategy is an aid to the circle or class meeting, **not** a substitute for it.

- Issues that are raised will either have short or long term solutions. The goal though will have only one direction – the enhancement of the quality of life for all members of the class, including the teacher, leading to an inclusive and empowering partnership in safety and learning.

- Issues will come from two different sources – you, and the pupils. Please remember that as a member of the class, you are as entitled as any pupils to raise an issue for action via the goal for the day. There is no reason that this should not be learning or classroom management goals.

- It is important that you ensure that the goals set are simple and achievable. Large issues brought out in circle time should be broken down into the constituent parts to make them manageable for the goal of the day. Small steps.

- "Goal of the Day" should also be used with some flexibility. If there is a "live" issue, then a goal towards solution should happen that day. This allows a quick level of response.

- No goal should carry punishment as a consequence of not being achieved. The goal is simply restated for the next day, perhaps with a smaller step planned.

- Always stress thoughtfulness and support as the way to achieve a set goal. This should help prevent bullying peer group pressure.

The Process

(a) In the morning...

- Settle the pupils down
- Announce it is "Goal for the Day" time under circle time rules.
- At the first time of including this strategy, explain why you are doing so and what you hope to achieve.
- Introduce an issue either from yourself, from the previous circle time or ask the pupils. There should be something of a balance in this. Nobody has the right to dominate the agenda in a partnership.
- Discuss with the class what the goal should be.
- Discuss the strategy for achieving the goal. It is not necessary, at this point, to name names. If one pupil is bothering another, for instance, then that can be the issue, and the goal is that this does not happen today. It may become necessary to name if the activity continues so that it is out in the open, and direct goals set for one pupil (supported of course by the other pupils who have some responsibilities as class members).
- Close the "circle".

(b) At the end of the day...

- Open the circle again.
- Ask, "Have we met the goal for the day?"
- If, after examining the evidence through discussion, the answer is "Yes", then offer congratulations and move to the "Supportive Pupil of the Day" award.

(Please refer to Appendix 2 page 39, "Active Displays and Support Certificates".)

- If the goal for the day has not been met, then it is necessary to discover why. This must be without seeking to blame, but by encouraging the taking of responsibility. The goal of support for those in need remains the guiding principle. The goal for the next day may be set here, to be reiterated the following morning. Then move to the "Supportive Pupil of the Day" award.
- If a goal is not persistently achieved because of a particular pupil's behaviour, this may be an indication that the pupil needs a support group. **Do not stay with a goal that is not being achieved for these reasons.** Set other daily goals, but remember to return because this is an inclusive strategy.
- Close the "circle".

Intended Outcomes

- A developing person and task centred classroom
- A developing mutually supportive classroom
- A warm and enjoyable classroom where education thrives
- A developing solution focused partnership
- The enhancement of emotional literacy and intelligence

(b) Support Groups

The model for these groups comes from the No-Blame approach to bullying. No-Blame seeks a solution to bullying by providing the victimised with a group of pupils who will offer them support. This would include the bullying pupil – though not identified as such to other group members, or accused of being a bully by the teacher or adult facilitating the group. When using these groups it was quickly realised that there was no reason that pupils should not support others, via the groups, in **any** area of need. The groups are a necessary accompaniment to the support code itself. In fact, historically, the support code was devised to support and sustain the work of support groups.

Support groups are an essential feature in the code strategy because:

- They can provide immediate and inclusive support for any pupil in any area of need.
- Rather than just talking about support and care, they allow all pupils to take a practical active role in the support of others.
- They encourage a solution-focused approach to problems.
- They encourage partnership as an approach to problems.
- They allow both the focus of the group and the pupils in the group to devise and own the solutions.
- They encourage the growth of empathy, emotional literacy and emotional intelligence.
- They can give confidence to parents because the school is acting on concerns rather than "monitoring".
- They can allow school and parents to act in a supportive partnership.

The method is quite simple...

Part 1: The initial meeting with the pupil who is to become the focus of the group

- Interview the pupil in need of help to discover as much as one can about the nature of the problem(s) being experienced.
- Suggest the use of a support group and explain how it works.
- If agreed, negotiate which pupils will form the group. This can be any number from 2-6 depending on the nature of the problem and the class/year group size. Flexibility is a key concept in all support group activities.
- It is important to allow the pupil who is the group's focus their own choices as well as making some of your own. All choices must be agreed.
- Agree with the pupil what may be revealed to the group.
- Invite the prospective group members to a meeting. Let them know that there is a pupil in need of help and they are being asked to support them. Do not, at this point, name the pupil.

Part 2: The initial meeting with the group

It has proved exceedingly effective to have the parents/carers of the "asking" pupil come to the first meeting of the group to act as advocates and ask for help for their child/young person. This also allows a proactive partnership between the school and parents/carers. If parents/carers can not do this, then it becomes the staff/volunteer role. The group focus is not asked to attend this initial meeting, though it may become desirable at future meetings.

- Thank the pupils for coming and explain to them again that they have been chosen as the most suitable pupils for supporting someone in need of help.
- The staff member/parent/carer should then state the nature of the problem and then identify the pupil in need. Support is then asked for.
- Prospective group members must be given the choice as to whether they want to offer support. Any pupil who does not, is thanked for coming to the meeting and allowed to leave.
- Before talking about the support strategies that may be offered, it is helpful to state the nature of the problem again. This both raises the level of empathy, and focuses minds.
- Ask the group members how they might help to improve the quality of life of the group focus. It may be necessary, especially with younger age groups, to input some adult suggestions.
- Make sure that they understand that the time scale for implementing agreed strategies is immediate. They begin as soon as the meeting is closed.
- Assure the group members that the adult facilitator (who is not necessarily a teacher) will be available to guide their support. Group members can request a meeting of the group at any time.

- Thank them for their intended support of somebody in need, and close the meeting.

Part 3: Monitoring the Work of the Support Group

It is important in the monitoring process to ensure that the goal of the group, to enhance the quality of life of the group's focus, is kept firmly in mind.

There are at least four monitoring opportunities for the facilitator of the support group:

- The **focus** of the group. This can be done easily by asking, periodically, if they feel they are being supported, and if they are feeling happier in school.
- The **group members.** This can either be by talking to individual members and asking for their thoughts, or through a formal group meeting: circumstances will dictate.
- **Parents/Carers** are an essential part of a monitoring process that also seeks a proactive partnership. So, a fundamental strategy for support groups involves inviting parents/carers into school, or talking to them over the phone, finding out if there has been improvements at home or if their child/young person is reporting being happier in school, or if the problem is not being sorted out.
- **Teachers and support staff.** Really this should say any adult in the school who might have contact with the focus of the group. Does the pupil seem happier? Are they getting on with their peers? Are they finding it easier to learn etc?

If it is discovered that problems are not being solved then the reasons must be found and brought to the support group so that new strategies can be considered.

Setting up a Support Group takes no more than 10-15 minutes. It needs to be noted however, that other problems may be revealed through the monitoring process and further meetings have to take place. Nevertheless, experience has shown that time invested is timed gained.

Groups run as long as the need is there. Some groups are dissolved after a couple of days while others have a long time span. Flexibility!

Intended Outcomes

- Pupils generally prepared to support other pupils in any area of need including behaviour management.
- A practical strategy for beginning the prevention of bullying rather than constantly having to react to it.
- A growing and inclusive partnership between staff and pupils
- A growing and inclusive partnership between pupils
- A growing and inclusive partnership between schools and parents/carers
- An enhancement of emotional literacy and emotional intelligence
- Happier pupils appreciating a more secure environment
- Productive communication

(c) Using the Curriculum

In many respects, the curriculum is the mainstay of sustaining the developing code and keeping its provisions in the foreground. With the introduction of Curriculum 2000 and the plans for Citizenship courses, this is an ideal time for a curriculum audit and review. There is some debate, which will undoubtedly continue, whether to teach Citizenship as a separate subject – a la PHSE – or have it fully integrated into National Curriculum subjects. It is of course possible to do both.

The support code strategy fits most easily into a cross curricula and spiral model. Apart from the early workshops, there are no plans for specific lessons except as a reinforcement and evaluation of progress - though the code can inform curriculum planning for separate Citizenship lessons if that is what a school chooses.

Any main developments in planning to integrate the support code into all subjects across the curriculum should take place in normal time allocated for such planning, however the teacher can be responsive to complimentary issues that arise on a daily basis...

- **By being aware of class/personal issues and using the lesson content to allow objective examination of the concepts involved. For instance, a teacher used a "Transport through History" project to consider the word "respect" by asking the pupils if they thought the Romans showed respect to the ancient Britons. A quick discussion followed with no real conclusion, but the concept of respect had been examined.**
- **The above was planned, but many issues arise via classwork and classroom management each day. Be an opportunist, but do not go in for overkill.**

The occasional reference to general code matters is part of the maintenance strategy. In such opportunistic moments, the displays become active in that parallels can be drawn.

● Some of these quick discussions might lend themselves to slogan making for future action statements because they highlight issues relevant to the class. This also continues the updating of active displays and action/code statements. Pupil volunteers can be asked to produce a slogan design, for instance, for a future area/concept to be discussed more formally during a circle time or via a PHSE/Citizenship type of lesson. Alternatively, if the issue needs immediate attention, it can be brought to Goal for the Day.

Some Examples of Curriculum Integration

These are real examples taken from schools that have piloted this work. It is important to note that the concepts under discussion, and integrated into the lesson, were provided by pupil responses to the initial and secondary code questions. This is how pupils both get their concerns taken up and contribute to the developing curriculum.

● **History** – Working Together: Studying the Tudors includes looking at how Lancaster and York had to come together to bring peace. Henry 7th invented the Tudor Rose as a symbol of 2 feuding families who had to come together to work for the betterment of all.

● **Science** – We Are All Different: Studying the body emphasises both similarities and differences. This is a good time to explore and explain that there are bits of our body we like and bits we don't like. It is easy to pick on someone for their sticking out ears or wearing of glasses etc, - but we all have things we don't want people to comment on, so we shouldn't do it to them.

● **R.E.** – Respect: Even within Christianity many people have different beliefs and they need to let everyone have their view. Respect is vital if Christianity is to survive.

● **Literacy Hour** – Support: " Susie the Dinosaur" is a story about giving help to someone in need of help even when they are a bully. Groupwork included pupils using their own experiences to write about times they have supported someone even when they have not liked them. Key words are explored for their meanings.

Appendix 1 - Forming the Circle

Introduction

Circle Time, and derivatives such as class meetings, is becoming increasingly recognised as an effective tool in helping pupils feel secure, and as a method for encouraging people to talk openly about their feelings. As such it is a more than useful tool for helping in the development of the support code.

Rules of the Circle

Rules of the circle vary from class to class and school to school. However there is a core of practice and purpose that is essential to using the circle. This includes:

- Sitting in a circle either on the floor or on chairs.
- The circle is essentially pupil time. As far as possible the pupils should set the agenda. It is their issues that are to be explored. This does not preclude the teacher having an input, and in the initial stages of working in the circle, the teacher must set the agenda.
- Only one person talks at a time. This is usually facilitated by the use of a "talking stick".
- Everyone pays respect to the speaker with the stick by listening to what they are saying and thinking about it.
- Everyone has the right to express their opinion.
- Everyone has the right to challenge the opinion of others.
- Everyone has the right to express their feelings.
- No one has the right to laugh at what somebody else says, but positive humour should always be encouraged.

Forming the Circle

This is the practical bit for when forming the circle for the first time.

- **Form a circle on the floor or in chairs. Pupils need practice at doing this! It is better for the first circle that you have set up chairs, or cleared a space on the floor.**
- **Talk to the class about the circle and what it is for.**
- **Tell them what your role in the circle is.**
- **Explain your circle time rules – for the first few circles this should form the first part of the circle. Eventually pupils will contribute to these rules.**
- **Introduce the talking stick.**
- **Introduce your first question and explain how you want them to answer it (including duplicate answers being ok).**
- **Pass the talking stick round the circle so that everyone can have a go. Don't make your first question a particularly serious one so that all can answer it. "How did you feel this morning when you got up?" or similar alternatives gives everyone something to talk about.**
- **Make sure you answer the question too – emphasising that you are part of the circle.**
- **Comment on some answers humourously, but only after all pupils have given their response.**
- **Ask your next question, starting on the opposite side of the circle to where you asked the first question.**

Handy Hints

- As facilitator of the circle, it is useful to exempt yourself from having to use the talking stick – otherwise a lot of time is wasted constantly getting it back to you! This should be explained to the class, and their permission sought for this arrangement. Majority rules!

- Do not allow the circle to go on for too long. Even older pupils have trouble sitting for the prescribed hour. 30 – 40 minutes is ample if pupils stay focused.

- Never form the circle without having things to talk about and explore in case the pupils do not have a topic.

- Don't always have serious circles. They can be used for game playing and having fun!

- A touchy subject is what to do with the pupil who breaks the circle rules and disrupts the circle. The most common practice is a yellow and red card system. If an initial, gentle, warning is ignored, then issue a yellow card. If this is ignored, then issue a red card. This means they have to leave the circle and cannot participate in the discussion. They sit outside the circle where they can listen but not participate. **This is time limited.** The circle is inclusive. 5 minutes is a reasonable length of time.

- Discuss with the pupils about what to do with those who disrupt the circle. This can be used to stress that the circle and support code are inclusive, supportive, strategies. The question is, "How do we **help** someone who wants to disrupt the circle"? Good idea to ask this question after explaining the circle time rules.

Appendix 2 - Active Displays and Support Certificates

Active Displays

There are a number of ways to raise awareness of anti-bullying and prevention of bullying issues, but the key to such work is how it is maintained. The first code questions generate a lot of display work – posters, poems, slogans etc. The intention is to actively use the displays rather than just have them as wallpaper. Reasons are:

● These displays are about how everyone wants to be treated by others, and, as such, are a constant and visual reminder of this.

● They can easily be referred to and used in conflict resolution and mediation.

● They can be used to generate circle time discussion.

● They can be used to help explore the social side of curriculum topics.

● Teacher/Pupil code answer displays help remind both of what has been discussed and agreed. They are essential for the development of action/code statements as they provide a record of sentiments expressed.

● Displays outside the classroom are a communication to other classes about the work that is going on.

The "Supportive Pupil of the Day" Award

This is an additional measure to support all the strategies encompassed by the support code and the school's behaviour management policies. It is easy to reproduce certificates and each class can design its own, using the computer, via a class competition. A number of different designs can be chosen for use. Friday assembly can be used to identify and award a school certificate, again designed by pupils, to the most supportive pupil in each class, nominated by the class teacher. A Head Teacher award, designed by staff, for the most supportive pupil in each year group, with corresponding certificate, would emphasise the whole school approach.

The elements in awarding the certificate are:

● Daily awards should involve both pupils and teacher making nominations and joint decisions.

● Do not award the certificate if there is nobody who deserves it.

● The certificate should state the actions for which it is being given.

● Five support certificates earns a letter home, and should be celebrated in assembly.

It is fair to point out that there is some disagreement concerning the use of "prize" certificates because, as the argument goes, they can become alienating for those who don't receive them, and confetti for those who do. The counter-argument would be along the lines of we are actively training our pupils in emotional literacy in the hope of sparking emotional intelligence: support certificates can reinforce this.

Appendix 3 - Continuing the Support Code on a Daily Basis

Introduction

The work of creating a safe and secure environment via the code does not increase the teacher's workload, but does ask for a thoughtful consideration of one's manner in the classroom. It also asks, for a particular approach to conflict resolution when problems are presented, and for the teacher to be alive to the possibilities of reinforcing the code, and developing it, through the daily curriculum.

(1) The Teacher's Manner

All teachers have their own style derived from their personality. Whatever your style, the following suggestions can help with maintaining the code...

- Always use please and thank you, and ask your pupils to do the same.

- Highlight good supportive actions.

- Make sure you keep to your side of the partnership negotiation from the first day. In other words, act on your own answers to the initial code questions. Encourage the pupils to tell you if you are not keeping to your side of the negotiation, just as you will refer to active displays when they are not keeping to their side.

- Put a ban on tittle-tattle after explaining the difference between that and a genuine complaint. One way to handle tittle-tattle is to ask, "Why are you trying to get A into trouble"?

- Demonstrate the kindness and consideration you are encouraging pupils to act on.

- A broken record approach is better than shouting. It allows for no deviation from your instructions, and can help to keep both you, and the pupil you are dealing with, calm.

- A handy non-shouting approach to bringing a class to order, from circle time, is to teach the pupils to respond to you putting your hand up, and them following suit and not talking with their hand up. Your hand is the signal for quiet rather than your voice. Pupils get used to this strategy quite quickly. You have to have initial patience with the stragglers! Looking in their direction is a practical ploy because others warn them.

- Never back a pupil into a corner, or cause a pupil embarrassment. These are poor disciplinary strategies.

- Be prepared to apologise if you are in the wrong. Apologise privately to the pupil you have wronged, and then tell the class what has happened. You are the role model. If pupils can learn to apologise, this will enhance the supportive atmosphere.

- Remember that you are the adult in all situations.

- Generally be a nice person, but remain firm when necessary!

(2) Resolving Conflict

Though each conflict situation is different, there are usually common elements that can be worked on. Mediation can take many forms, but never involves just skimming the surface as this leads to worse problems. Investing time in conflict resolution that works, saves time down the line. Using the ideas behind the support code, the following path may help to calm things down. It operates by putting each pupil in the other's place...

● Before discussing what the problem is, ask each pupil how they think the other pupil feels at the moment.

● Then ask each pupil how they actually feel.

● To get to the cause of the problem, ask each pupil **why** they feel that way.

● Tell the pupils you are not concerned with causes, but how to solve the problem.

● Ask each pupil in turn to say what they think the other would accept as the solution to the problem.

● Ask each pupil if the other has got it right, and what they might like to add.

● Agree a solution.

● Ask how each pupil is going to put the solution into practice, and ask if either thinks the participation of other pupils would be helpful.

● Whatever is agreed put into practice, but note down the agreement. It is essentially an action statement with an agreed goal that can be referred to if the initial attempt at conflict resolution fails.

● Speak to both pupils at the end of the day to see if the resolution has worked. If it has not, then the support of other pupils must be sought, perhaps via a support group.

● Asking at the end of the day shows you have not forgotten.

Some conflict issues between pupils, or lack of support by pupils, are whole class issues and should be put forward as resolution through goal for the day and even formal circle time. There does come a point, in the judgement of the teacher, where pupils causing problems can be named – especially when the problem, caused perhaps by bullying or classroom disruption, is like an open secret. This is **not** intended as naming and shaming, but rather to give a proper and open focus for support. Every member of the class is being encouraged to be responsible for helping others, and to take responsibility for harm they cause to others. **The class as a whole sometimes needs to work together to solve conflict and poor behaviour.**

Appendix 4 - Example of teacher and pupil responses to the initial code questions designed to develop a partnership between teacher and pupils

This is reproduced from one of the pilot support code projects. As prescribed, this was done on the first meeting with a Y4 class. The teacher's list had been prepared beforehand.

The Teacher Of Class 10 Says "Please..."

- Please always try to do your best.
- Please be happy in school.
- Please work hard.
- Please believe that you can do it if you try.
- Please be easy to get on with.
- Please be fun to be with.
- Please be kind to me, and everybody else.
- Please talk to me about any problem.
- Please do not be silly in your behaviour.
- Please do not do things that make me have to shout.
- Please don't be sulky. A smile is much better.
- Please enjoy being in the classroom with me.
- Please don't be nasty to each other.

The Pupils Of Class 10 Say "Please..."

- Please do interesting and enjoyable things.
- Please help us read.
- Please appreciate us.
- Please enjoy what we enjoy.
- Please help us with our spellings.
- Please help us with our problems.
- Please read to us.
- Please help us in all subjects.
- Please do surprises.
- Please do good displays.
- Please listen to our comments.
- Please show us respect.
- Please be kind to us.
- Please be polite to us.
- Please do not shout because people can't read.
- Please be fun.
- Please give us homework.
- Please be happy.
- Please help us when we're stuck.
- Please bring books to us.
- Please be nice.
- Please give us student of the week.
- Please tell us what to do.
- Please do not shout.
- Please be fair.
- Please give us rewards.

Appendix 5 - Example of pupil responses to the initial code questions designed to develop a partnership between the pupils

The Pupils Of Class 10 Say How They Think They Should Treat Others In the Class

- Treat people gently so they will not be sad.
- Treat them kindly because they have a right to a bit of kindness.
- With respect. Everyone has a right to be respected. We are all humans and should respect others - even people we do not like.
- Be helpful.
- Do not hurt their feelings.
- Always support people in everything they do, even if you don't like them.
- Always have time to listen to your friends, because they may have problems.
- Always remember your manners.
- I should treat others equally, because everyone is equal.
- Treat people with consideration, because other people's feelings are important.
- Be polite to people.
- I can be a bit more friendly to people around me and helpful by helping them if they are in trouble.
- Everyone needs kindness, support and respect.
- I want to have fun with people.
- Everyone needs friendship. If no one has friendship, everyone will be in a war.
- I should treat others with admiration when they do good ideas.
- Treat them how they treat me.

The Pupils Of Class 10 Say How They Want To Be Treated By Others In the Class

- With respect. People always bully you.
- Don't beat me up and make me afraid to tell my family or the teacher.
- Everyone must be supported in everything they do.
- Treat me kindly. People trip you or punch you on purpose and say sorry.
- I don't want to be hurt.
- Gently.
- Have fun with me.
- Have a laugh with me.
- Help me when I need it because everyone has the right to be helped by someone.
- Everyone has to be treated nicely.
- Be sensible.
- Be happy with me.
- If we don't have kindness, there would be loads of fights in the classroom and everyone would be hurt and nobody will be friends, and nobody will be happy.
- Don't bully me or leave me out of things.
- Don't tease or cuss me or say you're going to beat me up.
- Don't say things about my family.
- Listen to what I say.
- Be friendly. People aren't your friend because of your colour.

What should we do with the bully?

Children's understanding of what lies behind bullying is shown in answers below from children between 5 and 12 years old*. These answers are common - found again and again when children are offered an intelligent conversation about bullying behaviour.

> "They should find a buddy for the bully, to show her how to be a nice friend."

> "She feels sad - she needs to feel happy."

> "She shouldn't bully others even if her feelings are bad."

> "She should go to anger management classes."

> "Personal feelings from home make her take it out on Kelly."

> "But you're bullying yourself - we would listen to you if you didn't bully Kelly."

> "She doesn't have anyone to listen to her at home."

> "She might need to talk to someone about her problems."

> "She could phone Childline for some help with her problems."

> "It's' cos she's jealous - she might not have parents."

- Speak to the bully and see what help they need
- Ask the bullies why they bully

Questions

- Do you have a tough time at home?
- Are you jealous of Jay? (victim's friend).
- Do you feel lonely?

Suggestions to help

- Needs friendship
- 'Get anger management and people might like you 'cos you lose your toughness and maybe people would be your friend.'
- 'People might like you if you were a better person, and stopped being angry.' If you stop being tough, people will be nicer to you.
- A bigger girl might come and beat you up if you're not nice.

* These examples were collected during Camden Children's Fund work on bullying out of school, by Young Voice working with Kids Clubs Network, Chameleon Arts and Wax Lyrickal.

The legislative framework and messages from research.

The UN Convention on the Rights of the Child states that children and young people have the right to be protected from all forms of cruelty, torture and exploitation. In addition it also states that children have the right to an education which develops their skills and abilities, encourages them to respect their parents and their own and others' cultures. According to the convention, children have the right to leisure and play, to express their views and to have those views listened to regardless of their faith, race or culture.

Although the UK Government has ratified the UN Convention on the Rights of the Child it cannot be upheld in UK courts of law. However the European Convention on Human Rights is a relevant international legal instrument that is legally binding, hence it can be enforced in UK courts. The relevant articles in the European Convention are Article 3 (the prohibition of torture, cruel, inhuman or degrading treatment), Article 8 the (right to respect for private and family life) and Protocol 1 Article 2 – (the right to education)

Under section 61 (4) b of the School Standards and Framework Act 1998, headteachers are required to take action with regard to bullying: To encourage good behaviour and respect for others on the part of pupils and, in particular, prevent all forms of bullying among pupils. Section 175 of the Education Act 2002 places a duty on LEA's and governing bodies to safeguard and promote the welfare of children.

Guidance to promote children's welfare and protect them from abuse and neglect is contained in Working together to safeguard children. (DoH, Home Office and DfEE 1999) Reforms in the Green paper Every Child Matters (HM Treasury 2003) and Keeping Children Safe (DOH 2003) will take forward the recommendations from the Victoria Climbie report. (DoH & Home Office 2003)

The conventions along with existing legislation underpin the need to develop policies and practice to eliminate bullying where children and the adults working with them are understood, respected and listened to, and is free from exploitation, prejudice, cruelty and torture.

Creating a safe environment is everyone's responsibility. It requires commitment to ensuring physical safety and emotional wellbeing, thereby promoting emotional and social competence and positive relationships. It also requires developing inclusive policies that promote an understanding and respect for cultural diversity addressing all forms of prejudice and intolerance, including racism, sexism and homophobia.

Clear guidelines, policies and practice must also be established to promote emotional health and wellbeing and support children, young people and professionals. To prevent bullying, school communities need a range of responses in which children and young people are enabled and empowered to participate in the development of anti-bullying policies and strategies and take part in planning, development, dissemination and evaluation.

Research by Young Voice has repeatedly found that although schools increasingly have what they term an active whole school anti-bullying policy – the pupils may disagree; firstly on how widespread or embedded it is and secondly on how effective it actually is. (Bullying in Britain 2000 ; Fitting in or Fighting Back, 2002). We recommend that young people are helped to develop and own the ethos-changing and prevention of bullying work within the school community. We also recommend that anti-bullying work does not end at the school gate. Schools are urged to work with other services and groups recognizing that neighbourhood safety will enable pupils to feel safe and learn.

---

1 Adapted from Statement of Purpose, Anti Bullying Alliance NCB,NSPCC 2003

PREVENTING BULLYING: Helpful addresses.

Young Voice
25A Creek Road, East Molesey Surrey KT8 9EB

The Anti-Bullying Alliance,
8 Wakley St London EC1V 7QE
an alliance of over 50 organisations working together to
counter bullying. Further information about the alliance can
be found at www.ncb.org.uk/aba

Childline 08001111
freephone helpline for children

CHIPS Programme
45, Folgate St London E1 6GL, Childline in partnership with
schools programme.

Useful websites

www.antibullying.net

www.bullying.co.uk

www.dfes.gov.uk/bullying - includes 'Don't Suffer in Silence' and
the evaluation

www.eachaction@aol.com
Educational Action Challenging Homophobia

www.teachernet.gov.uk/safeschools

www.teachernet.gov.uk/streetcrime
(Safer Schools Partnerships).

www.schoolcouncils.org

www.wiredforhealth.gov.uk

www.young-minds.org.uk

www.youth2youth.co.uk

Stonewall – 'Safe for All' –
a good practice guide to prevent homophobic bullying by Ian
Warwick and Nicola Douglas, Institute of Education,
published by Citizenship 21
46-48 Grosvenor Gardens LONDON SW1W 0EB

Sport England
for guidance on inappropriate behaviour in sport.
16 Upper Woburn Place
LONDON WC1H 0QP

Children's Legal Centre for publication:
Bullying: A Guide to Law £4.95
www.childrenslegalcentre.com

Helpline for parents: parentlineplus 0808 8002222
Freephone helpline for parents

Millie's Fund – general safety www.amandadowler.com for
'Watch Over Me' 2003

Samaritans Tel 0345 909090
jo@samaritans.org

National Healthy School Standard
Health Development Agency
Holborn Gate
330 High Holborn
LONDON
WC1V 7BA

Lucky Duck Publishing Ltd
Books, videos and training
3 Thorndale Mews
Clifton
BRISTOL BS8 2HX

NSPCC
42 Curtain Road
LONDON
EC2A 3NH